No Missing Pieces

A Life Journey in Fragments

AUDREY BROWN LIGHTBODY

WESTBOW
PRESS®
A DIVISION OF THOMAS NELSON
& ZONDERVAN

WestBow Press books may be ordered through booksellers or by contacting:

WestBow Press
A Division of Thomas Nelson & Zondervan
1663 Liberty Drive
Bloomington, IN 47403
www.westbowpress.com
1 (866) 928-1240

ISBN: 978-1-9736-4532-0 (sc)
ISBN: 978-1-9736-4531-3 (hc)
ISBN: 978-1-9736-4533-7 (e)

Library of Congress Control Number: 2018913511

Print information available on the last page.

WestBow Press rev. date: 12/19/2018

Dedicated

in loving memory

to those who shared my journey

and

in living honor

to those who still share with me, the journey …

CONTENTS

INTRODUCTION

This is the life story of a very ordinary woman – it is the story of Audrey Brown Lightbody – a story told in fragments that make up the various parts of her life. It is unconventional in that it follows the journey chronologically, yet the contents in each section are disconnected fragments within the story - bits and pieces that fit into each fragment.

A significant resource played a part in my thinking as I worked on this memoir. Jigsaw puzzles came to mind. Doing these puzzles was always something I enjoyed. There are all of those scattered pieces that make up the picture in its wholeness. There are the four-sided edge pieces that give the puzzle a shape and make up the square. Within that determined edge there are many attributes that will make up the picture, but one must look for the fragments of color, of design, and even the way in which the pieces are notched. When, through trial and error, the fragmented pieces are put in the right order, one has a completed picture.

Jigsaw puzzles always have a picture on the box that allows you to do some matching up of the finished product. It is to be hoped that this puzzle is complete, without a missing piece or two. This memoir has no picture on a cover to help you – it is just fragments that through the years leads to this story of an ordinary woman, with the color and notches and design that create a unique person. The fragmented journey is written in prose and poetry and appears to leave "no missing pieces."

The reason for the subtitle comes from my five previous books – their titles make it very clear that both the words, *fragment and journey* are a part of most of the titles. Those previous books are all of a similar genre:

FAITH IS THE JOURNEY – *ESSAYS*
REFLECTIONS ON CARING FOR AN AGING
    PARENT – *LETTERS*
FRAGMENTED SENSES – *POETRY*
ORDINARY FRAGMENTS – *MEDITATIONS*
JOURNALING THE BYWAYS OF LIFETIME
    JOURNEYS – *JOURNAL*

Within the chronological fragments, there will be subject headings: Family, Home, Work and Faith Matters that are common to each segment but they all make up one continuous bit of poetry and prose within the lifetime journey- the jigsaw pieces, if you will. All speak of various parts of the journey of my lifetime and seem to culminate in this memoir using fragments of **NO MISSING PIECES** to finalize a fragmented story.

ACKNOWLEDGMENTS

Many, many thanks to **P**er Dahlin, who was a consulting voice in helping me over the hurdles in the preparation of this book.

The creations of my husband and children are shared by me, in deep humility for the wonder that they have added to my life.

Gratitude to Lenore Brashler, Alison Stendhal, and Judy Wallace, my technical advisor crew who made easy work of incorporating that which led to this final version.

My thanks to the many at West Bow Press who made this book a reality. They have carried me along and I am grateful.

The Beginning of the Journey -

Early Childhood

I Am Audrey

newborn child,

child of Ralph Jewell and Ethel Akerley Brown,

Child of God,

ready to experience

all the wonders of creation.

With a new unformed life, there are so many pieces afloat in the universe that need to be chosen and placed in some order as a life journey begins. Parents lay down the edge pieces that will shape the journey. They create the structure for the pieces that will be plucked from the many pieces available out in the universe.

The Beginning of the Journey

One of the fragments that is a part of my journey will, of necessity, be birth and the very early years. Under that heading, there is information that spells out who I am. I came as a new person. I was born at home, a not uncommon happening in those days.

I Am Called by Name

> "But now thus says the Lord; he who created you …
> do not fear, for I have redeemed you; have called you
> by name; you are mine".[1]

One of the first happenings in life is the choosing of a name. I had no part in the selection. My mother's best friend was an Audrey. I never met her, but I have often wondered what there was in friend Audrey whom my parents hoped might be a part of me. I will never know if I lived up to those expectations.

In doing some research on the Internet, I learned that there was a St. Audrey, also known as AEtheldreda. She was born in 626 in England and died in 679. She was the daughter of Anna, king of the East Angles, and Bertha. Her sisters were all saints of different areas in England. She was a princess, a Fenland and Northumbrian queen, and the abbess of Ely. She married at an early age to a prince for a few years. She believed God called her to live a life of virginity, and he allowed her so to do. After his death, she married Egfrid, son of the king of Northumbria, and continued to retain her virginity. With Egfrid's consent, she became a nun at Coldingham Convent. From there she returned to Ely, where she built a double monastery circa 672. She was abbess of the convent for the rest of her life and died there.[2]

I am certain that my mother, Ethel, never knew of that connection to Audrey. I am quite certain that I possess few of the saintly qualities of this royal and dedicated person.

Being called by name is important through all of life. There are many times that the call from God by name speaks of the ways such a call is heard and demands an answer.

In the Hebrew testament, God says "Moses, Moses" through the burning bush experience and called him to lead his people. (Exodus 3:4) God spoke to Elijah by name, asking him what he was doing in this place. Elijah was led to see God, not in storms of nature, but in the silence. The whispers of God called him to service. (1Kings 19:9)

Isaiah had a vision of God while in the sanctuary, of his lips being touched by tongs of fire and the voice of God saying, "Whom shall I send and who will go for us?" This was such a clear call to which Isaiah said, "Here am I. Send me." (Isaiah 6:8)

In the New Testament, we have the example of Jesus baptism and the confirmation that "this is my Son, the Beloved, with whom I am well pleased." (Matthew 3:16-17) Jesus was answering God's call. And there was Saul, who became Paul, struck on the road to Damascus by a vision of God asking "Saul, Saul, why do you persecute me?" Then God's call came with specific words about how to be a spokesman for God. (Acts 9:4)

These are but a few of the people who heard the call by name. Even in the many centuries gone by, there have been those who heard the call and replied, "Send me." (Isaiah 6:8)

This byway of thought seems like a diversion from the main facts of my early years. Yet it was important to put this hearing of the call, by name in this fragment, because it will become a major part of the story as I move on to the next parts of the journey.

Moving back into my early years, I need to say there is nothing new or startling that I can recall in those very early years. I learned there had been a child named Shirley, who was born before me and lived only a few months. This made me the older child who did not know much about this other child. How that loss of a child affected my family life, I would never know. There followed within two years, a younger child, my brother, Robert. All of this had little effect on me, but I did know I was cared for and deeply loved. I knew there were others in my life who helped me and were friends. All that most children do, I did: I grew, played, started learning about life. I was a happy, inquisitive child. I knew that Audrey was the loved child of wonderful parents.

I remember several instances in which the name Audrey had an impact on me. There was the time in my early school years in which there were the "Lil Audrey" jokes. It seems this Audrey either laughed and laughed or cried and cried over various circumstances. I was taunted with these stories. Fortunately this fad passed.

Other memories concerning my name belong farther along in my history, but the relationship fits with being called Audrey. In my high school homeroom there were three Audreys, all with last names that began with the letter B. We were the only students who had to have a full name called out to differentiate us.

In the retirement community in which I currently reside, there are also three Audreys. We all have different last names, but we are all women in our nineties. All of us have heard the call from God by name, and committed to lifetime journeys within the religious field of endeavor. We have responded to that call, saying, "Send me."

I Am Audrey

Child of God,

called by name,

uniquely me,

moving on into a journey

of remembering.

Moving on into a lifetime.

The Continuing Journey

Childhood to Young Adulthood

I Am Audrey Brown
Child of God,
child of Ralph Jewell and Ethel Akerley Brown,
learning to find my way
into personhood.

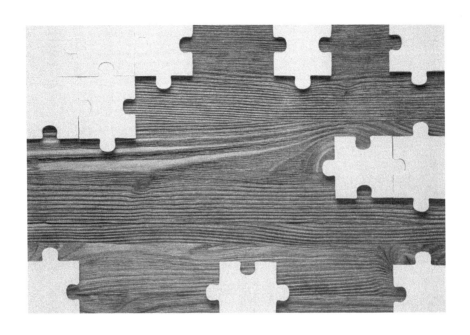

The puzzle has many pieces already in place as the journey continues. A variety of puzzle parts are added to a life. One never knows how many pieces have been looked at and even discarded when they no longer seem to fit. The puzzle shows us that there is much work needing to be done; many pieces yet to be added until the puzzle will unfold, until a life matures.

The first fragment in this continuing journey will, of necessity, be family. Family here means my nuclear family and I will briefly tell my story from my early years. This family gave me a sense of security and led me into the years of my life. I will begin each section with a poetic statement about the concept in general terms. I will follow it with parts of my life journey that are appropriate within those fragmented areas.

Family - A Continuing Journey

What is there about a family? What does being in a
*   family mean?*
We think about father, mother, and children
*   who live together, sharing a home,*
*   sharing life experiences, sharing in love.*
*   but family is so much more.*
Family goes back many generations, and we are
*   a part of that family who have influenced us*
*   in many ways;*
*   that family has spread out in extended ways into*
*   the present day.*
Family may be just two persons, one parent,
*   or older grandparents taking on the care*
*   of young children or being there for older children;*
*   or a group who gave loving care when it was needed.*
Family may also be in connection with an ethnic group,
*   a racial group, a religious group with no blood identity.*
Family may cover an entire world with people we will
*   never know.*

The family of God is made up of many "child's of God,"
   in fact, it does cover a whole wide world because
   a creating God shares our life experiences, shares
   in so much love that we are caught up
      in this God family in our own unique ways.

People Who Make Up Family

At this point in my story, I share with you some facts about my family. It consisted of my parents, Ralph and Ethel, and a younger brother, Robert, called Bob. As I tell of each of them, I must say that the Brown, and later, the Lightbody family, as well, was a very creative group. This creating attribute helped to define the family as each of us spent time creating beauty and sharing our creativity with others in our own unique way.

Ralph Jewell Brown and his parents moved to Boston; he lived most of his life in the Boston area. He was the youngest of three boys in the family, all who started their working lives in the Boston area. Telling about his working life is important to understanding the whole man. He had a variety of occupations: longshoreman, supervisor in a plating company, maintenance director at a church camp and conference center, and as office supervisor in a rug company. Even in retirement, he found ways to assist with housing concerns. The church was a vital part of his life. He held various positions as a layman in his local church and in the wider areas within the state offices of the American Baptist Churches USA. All he did within the church was his way of giving service to his God.

Dad had a green thumb and made all the grounds of their homes into little islands of beautiful gardens. He loved having fresh produce from his gardens: tomatoes and salad ingredients were always fresh and tasty. He even helped us, as Ralph and I moved from church to church, to find loveliness in our garden arrangements.

Ethel Akerley Brown

My mother was also born and lived her early life in Canada. Both of them were from New Brunswick. She came with her parents as a bride to the Boston area. In my younger years, my mother stayed at home but did some outside jobs to add to the family finances. In my teenage years, Mother took a job as office manager in a real estate agency. Mother was front and center in her contributions to the local church, sharing her faith and devotion to God through numerous ways of service. In later years my mother accepted positions as a laywoman with some authority within our denomination. Mine was a family committed to stewardship as a response to God's call.

I believe my writing ability stemmed from my mother's creativity. Mother wrote dramas that were presented in her church and in programs nationally that were a part of Women's Groups within their churches; even in her later years she edited and wrote an in-house newspaper for the retirement home where my parents lived. My mother wrote as she lived – in response to God's call.

Robert Ralph Brown (Bob)

Bob was born two years after me and I became the older child, who enjoyed having a younger brother to whom I could show love. As a family we were pretty average; we did school and church and found friends for each of us. As we were growing, I often felt the need of protecting this brother, however, that relationship became problematic as we matured, having the usual squabbles and differences. Although various things seemed to cause separation between my brother and me, we knew we were tied with bonds of love that could survive whatever would come. As adults, we became very close and knew that that love was a powerful force in our lives.

A capsule view of his life involved service in the Army, a marriage, begetting five children, a divorce and a second marriage. He worked as the manager in a specialty store; became an entrepreneur in his own businesses. His wife, Edna, was a working partner. I noted previously, that creativity was a part of our family. My brother went to art school and developed his artistry to the place where he had a reputation and many showings of his work. He even donated a large piece of art to the RIDES for Bay Area Commuters office where it graced the entrance lobby. He was a man of great creativity.

Home– A Continuing Journey

While family reached beyond just the primary group, I noted that much of my family life took place within the houses where we lived. These houses, that were really homes, became a part of my journey. I share with you yet another fragment: Home.

What is a home? What changes a house into a home?
In one's lifetime a family may live in many houses,
>*in many places, even in the wider world;*
>>*are all of these "homes?"*
The decorations, the living arrangements may change,
the climate may be different, friends are not as near,
neighborhoods are not as familiar;
>*can all of these changes be a part of home?*
Home is where the heart is, shared by all who live

within its walls:
caring, giving and receiving love,
living within the warmth of each other.
Home is where we learn life's lessons.
Home is where we grow into personhood;
Home is where we grow in our knowledge of God,
and God's love for each member of the family.
Home allows us to become the persons
God calls us to be!

Home for the Brown family was a movable feast. Somerville, a suburb of Boston, was the place. In my first years, including all of my elementary school years, we moved four times within the same city. All of these houses were rentals, but for me all of them were "home." They were safe places in which to be loved and nurtured and learn to be a happy child. School, church, friends and neighborhood, all contributed to my growth. My grandmother came to live with us when I was five years old and this added a new dimension to our household. My grandmother, on my mother's side, did dressmaking, so I was assured of always having great clothes to wear. Her divorced husband lived a distance away, but close enough that he would come to visit us. My other grandparents, on the Brown side, lived across the city in Allston, and this meant a Sunday trip by subway to visit them. Grandpa Brown was a retired sea captain and he had interesting tales to tell about his life with three-mast ships. This was also a warm-hearted home.

From the peripatetic moves, the family lived in the same house through Junior High and most of Senior High school. It was a time of stability; school and study years, family joys and deep friendships that lasted many years. All of these were building blocks for a future that depended on everything in life that had gone before. These years were a time of learning that life is not always rosy. There was illness, death, and opportunities for challenge in the homes that made up the journey. All of these were along a known track, with little blips along the way that called for making adjustments within the journey.

In the ninth grade I wrote my first real poem and thus began my career as a writer.

WANDERINGS

I wandered far away one night
from jangling noise and foolish care,
out where all was calm and peace
and joy was everywhere.

Where all men did as brothers live
and envious strife did not there reign,
where everyone another helped
the highest to obtain.

But, alas, I woke and found myself
amid the same old noise and care,
but in my soul one purpose great,
to help all love and share.

My writing continued with a drama that was presented at several local churches and even in my English classroom, in my high school. That poem and the drama were consistent with my journey. It grew out of a family and a home life committed to seeking God's will. We understood that we were called to be co-creators with God in the work of the world. In those years I developed independence, was a happy scholar, was into all of those things that teen-agers did (probably some not so good).

My family's journey led us all into a new situation. This was a big blip on the family journey. It was one that required my brother and me to understand that a straight, uninterrupted track is not entirely possible. The family moved from the place that had been home in Somerville to a different city, Melrose. My parents owned their first home and it was to be "home" in a special way. This move came just as I would begin my senior year in high school. This presented several challenges: how to break into a school where I was an unknown from the security of being at the top of my class, how to have new friends who might only be such for a short time. I looked ahead into my college years. What about God's plan for my life – how would I know?

Who would have thought that my years of being in a summer "School of Methods" a Christian summer camping program for high school age students, would be a part of the answer? In my new church in Melrose, I found there were several girls who had been my friends in that program. They immediately scooped me up and suddenly I was with a recognized group, both in church and in school. My friend, Betty was at the forefront of this group who included me. Even today, Betty and I have maintained our friendship, though living across the country from each other. This friendship, in our later years, was the sort that included both of our families and many trips together and deep, deep roots of love.

God works wonders and led me into next steps on my journey. One of the continuing fragments involved a part of life called Work. Here too, I make my statement and tie it into my journey.

Work – A Continuing Journey

What is work? Why do I work? Is work a necessity in life?

> *One works for money – to pay bills;*
>
> *to purchase necessities, to find joy in fun and activities.*

Why do I work – to fill up time – long hours in a day,

> *to find others who share a common need within the 24 hours,*
>
> *to learn and to advance knowledge in a given field,*
>
> *to find ways of helping others in their journey,*
>
> *to be God's worker wherever the journey leads.*

Is work a necessity in my life? I say "yes" because

> *work gives meaning in my inmost being as a child of God.*

On my continuing journey, I did prosaic things such as working in a Woolworth's store in the summer and on Saturdays year round from my mid-teens. I did babysitting for neighbors and helped with things at home. As I progressed in my later high school years, I also worked in a department store, again on Saturdays and in the summer.

While I was working through my feelings about where God would lead me, God's call caused me, during high school years, to work as a volunteer at a Christian Center in the north end of Boston. I was busy helping with Vacation Church School and some other activities within the Center, as time allowed. I was working with a good many Italian families and was learning about people from other cultures. This service continued in the summers when I was home from my college days.

The fourth fragment is one that undergirds the journey in its entirety. Faith and its meaning has become a central core in my life. It is not separate from the other fragments. Faith binds everything else into one whole so that I moved ahead, having God as a part of me.

Faith Matters – A Continuing Journey

What is faith? How do I acquire it?
The Bible tells us about faith:

> *by faith Abraham moved out into a new land,*
> > *trusting in God's promises.*
> *Paul reminds Timothy of the faith of his mother*
> > *which is now imbedded within him.*
> *Faith can be as small as a tiny seed and yet*
> > *it can grow into a life-giving force.*
> *Faith is the belief that things unseen,*
> > *by our human eyes,*
> > *bespeak a God who lives in the world.*
> *Faith, hope, love, and service are gifts in our lives;*
> > *to be a part of each of us in trust from God.*

What does faith mean in my life?

This next fragment is called Faith Matters. There is a double entendre within that fragment. It can be the various issues of faith pulled into one general title or it can be what it says that faith matters within one's life. It is a crucial part of the journey.

My family, as noted, was deeply religious, teaching us about faith, and a loving God. My parents helped my brother and me to understand about God and what being a child of God would mean in our daily lives. Church was an important part of my growing up years. Family devotions were a part of my life. In this home atmosphere I grew to understand that all people were a part of God's plan. Color or church affiliation did not matter; we were all equal in God's sight. I was blessed to have parents whose faith led them to be in the forefront of social justice.

Both my parents were leaders in church life in each of the churches of which they were a part. Naturally, we grew up understanding that we, my brother and I, must share in church life and in extended service outside the boundaries of family and home.

I remember in the depression years that we were people who got along with what we had, not probably even middle class. I recall my mother feeding people who came to our home begging for food. This was all a part of her belief of the importance of following the Christ to whom she had committed her life. There were other examples of my parents who trusted God to lead them. To tell of this would demand more time than this fragment would allow.

Now ready to be college bound, I was answering the call of God to find my way into committed service. Trying to be in God's will led me to attend the <u>Baptist Missionary Training School</u> (BMTS) in Chicago, Illinois, so that I could prepare to work in church-related ministries. BMTS was a Christian woman's college in a city (Chicago) with many problems and many opportunities. Students, as a part of field education, were able to work in needy places and in churches, as a part of their training for service.

In my two years there, I learned, as a student, not only the educational requirements, but how to sort out the way to what my adult years could be. These were years of new and lasting friendships, learning wisdom about myself and how to serve God. All of this caused me to truly become Audrey Brown, my own person, child of God.

I Am Audrey Brown

Child of God

from earliest years,

college student – into a world

far from home and friends,

on my own, daring to find my place,

awaiting where God and life

would lead me next.

A Turn in the Journey

A New Family Journey

I Am Audrey Brown Lightbody
Child of God,
wife of Ralph Homer Lightbody,
partner in ministry,
lover of each other
lover of family
lover of life.

Jigsaw puzzles can be a time of sharing. Many hands can try to fit pieces into the puzzle. Trying to work together as a family unit has the possibility of being frustrating or joyous. The puzzle may reflect the color and design of each of the persons who share the journey. It is often necessary to turn the puzzle to get the full effect of its wholeness and to see it in new ways. The turns in life are also a way to understand the journey.

Here the story changes. I have taken a major turn in my life. I have left the straight ahead road, as it was early perceived, and found a different pathway that changed me and my journey. It also caused disruptions in the perceptions of Family. As before, I begin this section with a poetic statement about this turning point in the journey. I will follow it with parts of my life journey which are appropriate within those fragmented areas. In addition, there will be extensive poetry that is a major part of that period of my life.

Family – A Turn in the Journey

What is there about a family? What does being in a
      family mean?
Family is continually in change, additions and subtractions;
         change within its members as the years come and go,
         change within the outreach among its members,
         changing perceptions about the place within the family
            of all who make up the family unit.
The intermingling of families as new family units take place;
         learning how to fit as a member of two families,
         knowing where one fits in the newer family schemes.
Now there are families within families who have to
         learn how to be in fellowship with many others.
The family of God is made up of many, many families;
         in fact, it does cover a whole wide world because
         a creating God shares our family experience,
         shares in so much love that all families
            are caught up in this God family
            in their own unique ways.

While this was a turn in my life, it was not an unexpected route in many life journeys. I fell in love and that event caused a significant change in my life. It meant turning my thoughts into thinking about marriage and a new family that might yet be. It meant spending hours in preparation for my marriage and plans for the future that will not include as much time for my nuclear family. It meant also, that I would need to be aware of and, in my activities, be a part of another family – Ralph's family. The word family now has multiple meanings and requires a degree of intentionality as I pondered the turn in my journey. It also was a year of waiting. It was a time for writing about my feelings as a part of my faith journey. It was a year filled with boundless love on all sides and from so many people.

WILDERNESS WANDERINGS

I am apart
alone in wilderness wanderings,
looking for the dew-drenched fleece,
seeking the burning bush,
listening in the sheer silence,
listening, listening ...

I am a part
of others in the wilderness wandering,
sharing in the seeking,
being in the sharing,
desiring the hope,
waiting for the silence
to speak ...

Apart and yet a part ...
the Eternal Holy One

listens to me, to us,

speaks to me, to us

> in the silence,

> in the hope-filled minute,

> in the sharing

> in the wilderness wanderings.

People Who Make up Family on the Turn of the Journey

It is important to share a bit about the people who were among the family unit that would become "family" in a real sense. I begin with my husband to be and then tell about his parents

Ralph Homer Lightbody

Ralph was an only child of older parents. They, too, had lost a child in their early years, before Ralph was born. As was true with my family, there is no record of how that affected the family. It did mean that Ralph was a dearly loved only child. Their home in Roslindale was the only home that he knew from birth to his marriage to me. Home was a secure, safe place filled with much love. He had a different childhood than that experienced by the Brown family. He did not know how life went on with siblings. This was to affect him as we had children who did the usual squabbling.

Ralph went to Gordon College where he received his BA. After receiving a call from God, he answered "yes" and decided that that call was to be in the ministry. He went on to Andover Newton Theological Seminary in Newton, Mass. where he earned his Master of Divinity degree (then called Bachelor of Divinity). Many years later, within our marriage, Ralph earned a Doctor of Ministry from San Francisco Theological Seminary in San Anselmo, California.

The rest of his life will be spelled out in our joint journey.

Homer and Marion Lightbody

Ralph's father had an ice and oil business and his mother was a stay at home parent. They too were from Canada. Ralph was loved and cared for and taught great values that lasted him a lifetime. His parents also saw to giving him training in singing (he had a marvelous baritone voice) and playing musical instruments, all of which were a very deep part of who he was. They, too, were a religious family, making his love of faith and witness as a cornerstone in his life.

Home – A Turn in the Journey

What is a home? What changes a house into a home?
In one's lifetime a family may live in many houses,
in many places, even in the wider world;
are all of these "homes"?
Moving means that there must be adaptations
for each family member, for the interplay
among the family members,
for growth at different levels for each person.
A house where love flows constantly can be a home,
no matter where it is located,
for all who live within its bounds.
Home allows us to become the persons
God calls us to be!

Work – A Turn in the Journey

What is work? Why do I work? Is work a necessity in life?
*Work **is** a necessity in my life!*

> *it is in work that I find my calling,*
> *it is in work that I find fulfillment,*
> *in work that I help to actuate God's plan*
>> *for me and also for those who come into my*
>> *care.*

There were reasons for me not to return to BMTS and for me to spend a year living in my parent's home, while Ralph lived at the Seminary and continued his education.

In that year, prior to our marriage, I found a wonderful job close to my home. Through the kindness of the Director of Christian Education in Massachusetts, I found a position at a neighboring church as Secretary/Christian Education leader. I was able to use my skills learned at college and serve in ministry. It was a fulfilling year of work.

Family Matters – A Turn in the Journey

What is faith? How do I acquire it?
What does faith mean in this new place in our shared journey?
We have moved into a place where we will lead

> *into new areas of service, new commitments.*

We do so, trusting in God's promises.
We bring the combined faith lessons from two families

> *and merge them into a unity for this family.*
> *We trust that all of the seeds planted*
> *will have grown into a strong life-giving force.*
> *Faith, hope, love, and service are gifts in our lives;*
> *are a part of each of us in trust from God.*
> *Faith and belief are deep within our lives.*

The Pathways in the Turn in the Journey

I met Ralph while in high school, through numerous Association Youth meetings that covered the Boston area. He was a well- known figure in many of those gatherings. He also attended the School of Methods where we shared that experience in Ocean Park, Maine. In the time of our engagement, we both, in separated male and female facilities, were tent leaders for the younger people.

I married Ralph Lightbody, my love, a seminarian with one year left to complete in his seminary training. Thus began a journey of continuing love as a family of two and how much more was yet to be. The next part of the story will combine, as one piece of the whole, the *family*, the many *homes* within our fifty four years of marriage, varying *work* opportunities and always *faith matters*. It is hard to note the differences between family, home, work and faith matters for they were so integrated in those years of the turn in the journey. This was true even in the movements we made to different state locations while serving in ministry. I would note that Ralph's call to the ministry and my call to ministry meant that our partnership was always about answering the calls we both felt from God.

Such calls were deeply entrenched in faith matters. We were so blessed to be called to wonderful pastorates which were a part of our world view and not limited to tightly restricted conservatism. These churches permitted us to grow in our faith and expand our need to witness for the God whom we served.

A very important part of our faith call had to do with the inclusivity of all people, regardless of race and national origin. I grew up in a church that had Filipino and Black members. My mother and father belonged to a group known as the Color Caravan, a mixed racial group, which went to other churches and spoke of the need for inclusion within the Church. Ralph and I also had close friends of a variety of races, so inclusivity was vital as we considered the calls from the churches we would serve.

While the churches to which we were called were largely white congregations, an important part of the ministry was finding ways to be inclusive. Since this was an important part of our call, there were a variety of ways to assist those churches to understand more fully that everyone is a loved child of God.

This happened in a variety of ways among the pastorates. In one church, Ralph led the congregation to hire a Black Associate Pastor. In another church, we developed a sister relationship with a mostly Black church. We, as a congregation, had very meaningful times of worshipping together and social interaction. In yet another church, we developed a program of working with inner city churches in a children's program that permitted close relationships socially with people of different races. For the churches' children, this became a way of growing into deeper meanings of faith. These activities were all a vital part of leading our congregations to understand a God who loved all people. Our family life was enriched as we included people from around the world as brothers and sisters in the one God.

Every pastorate had both its joys and sorrows and even moments of stress. We found that not only in the joys, but even in conflicts and challenges, that which led us into growth and strengthened our faith. This caused us to look into how our faith matters could work within our congregations as well as in our lives.

Sharing bits of all these fragments, I will enunciate them within the various homes in which we lived. These homes are all identified by the pastorates in which we served, reaching from New England to California and into retirement. Work will be named for the family members as we journeyed together over forty plus years. All of this movement, as family, made up of years of loving, being loved, and offering love to so many people. These were all a part of the journey, along with the rest of our family.

CAROLINA, RHODE ISLAND – 1948

While attending seminary and in our first year of marriage, Ralph held a student pastorate in Carolina, Rhode Island. We lived in the parsonage of the church and commuted back and forth to Seminary in Newton Centre, Massachusetts during the week. We had connections with our two families in this time while Ralph finished Seminary. Our small family of two was a part of both of our families in very real ways – some meals, some nights in one home or another, but always maintaining our identity as a family. It was a time in which we sorted out what would be demanded of us as we began this turn in two journeys, but now a melded one. While Ralph was working and studying, I worked in a nearby candy shop, thus adding to our limited income.

This was a time in which we struggled with how we would develop spiritually as we tossed the many balls of our life. Family devotions was a practice that we needed and would continue throughout our lifetimes.

Personally, I craved the silence as times to be still and know God.

Bible passages and words from hymns led me into the presence of God. I sought refuge from the everydayness of life, from the stresses of hatred, from my own willingness to be less than God called me to be. In the book, *THE MESSAGE*, edited by Eugene Peterson, I found contemporary words, in a variety of verses from Psalms 61, 62, 63 that I used as a mantra within the silence, wanting it to lead me further into God's plan for my life.

"God, listen to me shout,

bend an ear to my prayer.

You've always given me breathing room,

a place to get away from it all,

A lifetime pass to your safe-house,

an open invitation as your guest.

You've always taken me seriously, God,

made me welcome among those who know and love you.

God, the one and only----

I'll wait as long as he says.

Everything I hope for comes from him,

so why not?

He's solid rock under my feet,

breathing room for my soul,

An impregnable castle;

I'm set for life.

God said this once and for all;

how many times

Have I heard it repeated?

'Strength comes

Straight from God,'

God-you're my God!

I can't get enough of you!

I've worked up such hunger and thirst for God,

traveling across dry and weary deserts.

So here I am in the place of worship, eyes open,

drinking in your strength and glory.

In your generous love I am really living at last!

My lips brim praises like fountains.

I bless you every time I take a breath;

My arms wave like banners of praise to you."[3]

In addition to my planned quiet time, I made use of the travel time of getting to and from work to be in conscious time spent with God. I could be still and listen in the silence.

With the completion of seminary and the student pastorate, we moved into full-time as a married couple with a new pastorate, still in the State of Rhode Island.

WAKEFIELD, RHODE ISLAND - 1949

Our home in Wakefield was in a parsonage right next door to the church, which included a cemetery on the grounds. The family at this point, was just the two of us. We learned about what marriage entails and how love can grow. Another learning was how to be pastor and wife to a wonderful congregation and how to give full time service to those who had a need of us. We chose to make this home a place where all felt welcome. We entertained, in addition to church members, those from far and wide within the areas around us, even within the state. It was a good period in our lives, where Ralph served as a great pastor to this church of two hundred plus members.

Since this is my story, I will not go into great detail about Ralph's ministry. He was a great pastor, a sound theologian, a real shepherd to, not only his church flocks, but in outreach within the denomination and interfaith matters as well.

As the church grew, it became necessary to do some additions to the church building. For a couple just out of seminary, it was unique to be presented with this challenge so early in ministry. The architect who worked with us indicated that it probably spoke of what might happen in future church ministries. This did indeed became a pattern in most of the churches we served.

It is important to say that even in mundane matters, faith mattered for Ralph wherever he was – this was my beloved. God was in every part of his being.

In these six years in the Wakefield Baptist Church, we developed our own shared decisions in faith matters. Daily devotions at the start of the day became a must in our family life as we sought God's guidance for each day. Each of us created our own meditation practices done during the day. Evening brought us again to time with God and the consigning of the night into God's love. We became avid searchers for ways to understand God's will for our lives. We were blessed as we spent time in meditation, not only by ourselves, but also with groups of people. Faith mattered then, and still does today.

Within a few years, (1954) we added to our family with the adoption of our beloved daughter, Joyce Elaine, into our home. Needless to say, home tasks increased, as did the joy that was filling our home. Having a charming daughter in our home, only made everything more special. In those years I stayed at home, being the pastor's wife, and using my talents for our church and the state regional offices.

I did not work outside the home It was in being a pastor's wife that I sensed that all work is not the paid for variety. I did give myself to working in church related activities within our state and association duties. I carried some major responsibilities in Christian Education and Women's Work within our denomination, the American Baptist Churches USA. Drama productions with the young people and adults in our church was a new talent that I worked on in those years. Developing small groups within our church was a talent forged in this church and continued through all of my ministry. As a volunteer in our churches and in my work in the larger area, I was able to work, at home, using my writing skills in a paid capacity. In those years, I wrote curriculum for church school, and developed written programs for youth groups, all within my denomination. Work was at home, allowing for caring for our family and its values.

Faith matters influenced the pathway we took in training our young child, so that she would understand that God was a member of our household. Our own growth in faith, love and service guided us through these years.

LYNN, MASSACHUSETTS – 1955

Our family, now three, moved to a new home in a parsonage in Lynn when Ralph responded to a call to be senior pastor at the Washington Street Baptist Church. It was almost like returning to my early home, since Lynn was very close to Melrose, just a few miles apart. That meant being close to my birth family and so expanding our family again. Ralph's parents lived farther away and his mother died while we were in the early years of our move to Lynn.

Our family increased again with the adoption of a child from

Greece – Keith Alan (1955). He was a happy, quite contented child in those very young years, unlike his older sister who was always on the go. Our family was secure within the larger church family. While the parsonage was our main home, we purchased our first home on our own: a summer home in Bristol, New Hampshire. This became our vacation spot for most of our vacations. This home was a treasure for our family of four. My Brown family enlarged with the marriage of my brother and the addition of five children to that union. Family now included more than one family: our parents and assorted cousins, plus my brother's family. We were blessed to have Ralph's father visiting for brief times, for a few years, but he passed on within a very few years. Our children have no memories of Ralph's parents and so lost some of that sense of family that might have been. For our family of four it was a great time, still having loving grandparents from the Brown side of the family. Ralph's working ministry expanded and we again added on to the church facility in a small building on the property. With a larger church and new tasks Ralph always allowed for time in our home and with the children. It was an essential part of his ministry. Again our home was always open to all groups and friends from near and far. In addition we were both active with state and association leadership.

My working life continued much as it had been in Wakefield. I wrote a play for a denominational magazine, in addition to my other writings. My volunteer work included writing dramatizations for our church and for our state woman's work. Drama and small group development again called for my leadership in the church. With each new task, I gained in my faith and understanding of God's plan for my life.

Faith and commitment to our tasks at home, at work and in family, were a large part of our faith matters. We continued to be seekers of God's plan as we answered the call of God. Family devotions continued as before as we helped our children, even at their early ages, to understand how blessed we were to be in God's loving care.

DREXEL HILL, PENNSYLVANIA – 1959

Much of the story in the turn of the journey takes place here. We had a pastorate in the Drexel Hill Baptist Church for fourteen years. This was home, the place where the children did all of their schooling from grade one through high school. How blessed our family was for the stability of this location.

Our home was again a parsonage, but wonderfully functional for our family and its many pursuits. It was in this home that family events, work for all of us, and faith matters found fruition. Being close to the national offices of our denomination at Valley Forge meant that there were opportunities for both Ralph and me to serve on national committees for the American Baptists.

We continued to love being at Newfound Lake in New Hampshire for our vacations, even though it was a nine hours journey each way. We traveled in late afternoon and into the evening so that the children could sleep on the way. It *was* easier than trying to keep them entertained for those long periods.

Ralph did his ministry in this church of 700 members, training Associates and working with Seminary students as they embarked on ministry. Here the church building required that we have more dealings with an architect. We built a Chapel, with a beautiful spire, as an addition to the lovely church on a main street corner. Ralph also served as Adjunct Faculty at a local junior college. He too, did some writing of hymns that fitted the needs of the congregation.

Illness was a part of our lives. I had a life threatening illness with intestinal gangrene that required extensive surgery and required a significant amount of time in rest and recuperation. Fortunately, this occurred prior to my working outside the home. Major changes were called for and the family adapted.

At a later time, both of the children contracted serious different illnesses, at the same time, and this required tumultuous adaptations; so while family was still real, it happened in different locations. We had one child in the hospital with rheumatic fever and a child at home with a strain of meningitis. We could not bring our daughter, Joyce, home from the hospital because of the danger of infection from Keith's illness. One member of our church family took in our daughter, with me being there every day to do the necessary tasks. Ralph stayed at home with our son, while carrying on his pastoral duties. Love reached out from so many directions. Surviving all of these illnesses enriched our family and helped in our trust of God's loving care. We hoped that growing up in a place where love was shown would lead our children into trusting in the power of love.

Divorce was also a part of those years. My brother and his wife separated and while they lived in the same city, the children lived with their mother and Bob had them on weekends. When several years later, Bob remarried, we added a new member to our family. Fortunately, Bob's children lived between two homes that were nearby, and so life went on.

Within the church itself my work continued in its same pattern: writing, drama, entertaining, developing small groups, finding ways to work for justice and teaching. A learning disability with our son, found out in the fifth grade, made it necessary for us to send him to a specialized school as he entered the intermediate years. Then it was that I went to work outside the home and it became a pattern for the rest of my working years. I need to say that the volunteer work continued in all the areas mentioned, for the rest of my working life.

I began by working in a local Seminary Library, moved on to working for the University of Pennsylvania as an administrative assistant. I left that position after a few years and went to be an Administrative Secretary, working in the Department of Christian Higher Education in the denomination. In this capacity I worked as a volunteer with the National Campus Ministry Association. There were other national committees that used my talents and called for me to do some traveling. I was careful never to let this work override my commitment to my family and my church.

My time with the Baptists took another jog as I became a Customer Services Representative for Judson Press, the publishing arm for the denomination. I learned a lot about printing and used my writing skills in this area as it was needed. At the time we concluded ministry in Drexel Hill, I concluded my working relationship with the offices in Valley Forge.

Work became a household activity as Joyce and Keith became old enough to take on jobs befitting their age and ability to perform specific tasks. Joyce had a variety of different jobs while she was in high school: working in a department store, doing telephone sales, waitressing, and serving in a dentist's office. Keith had a paper route and pumped gas at a local gas station; there were probably others that I don't recall, in both children's cases. Of course, these were done on Saturdays and in the summer months.

This amount of work activity among all of us caused major shifts in our normal living schedules. Home, family and work created a new normal within the family and caused us to understand that changes had to be made. We tried to be constant and growing in matters of faith. Faith and our relationship with God became a two pronged approach: how could we best help our children believe in a God of love who would be with them all their days; how we, as parents, would go more deeply into faith matters for ourselves. It was important for our children to understand that faith and belief were a life-long process.

Ordinary living was about every day in which we tried to live out our Christian faith as a family in our home. While there were many seasons and much delight in the ways we dealt with the variety of seasons, I have chosen the Christmas season for giving special thought to faith matters. I suspect that my poems tell far more of my own private thoughts than of the family. Christmas and all of its joy was always a blessed, happy family and faith-filled time. It was important to assure us all that Christ was in this time and that our children should know the love of God coming in the Christmas miracle.

CHRISTMAS HOLIDAYS

Rushing, rushing – so much to do:
> decorating at home, Christmas trees,
> how I clothe myself.
Rushing, rushing – so much time spent:
> preparing cookies, goodies,
> parties for friends, spectacular meals.
Rushing, still rushing, so much money:
> gift giving for work, for friends,
> for family is it enough, too much?
Rushing, rushing – so little time:
> to give thought to just living,
> everydayness with family.
Rushing, rushing – so little time to
> fit in what the season means,
> to be within my church in this time.
Rushing, rushing – no time guides us

through the days and weeks and hours,

that lead to the birth of the Holy Child.

CHRISTMAS HOLIDAYS

Glittering, glittering – everything about these days

is subsumed in glittery tinsel and miniature lights,

in resplendent jewels to add sparkle to it all.

Glittering, glittering – tradition calls us to make it so:

gifts wrapped with large silver bows,

candlelight inside and decorations to outshine another.

CHRISTMAS HOLY DAYS

Glittering, glittering – only the ordinary:

starlit skies so clear that one

could see a single star to guide the way.

Glittering, glittering – only the ordinary:

the music of the spheres, as the world turns;

angel songs that light the birth of the holy child.

HOLIDAYS AND HOLY DAYS

In the rushing, let us hear the plodding of the first holy days:

let us leave the tumult of the things to be done,

and walk more slowly the way that leads to the holy.

Amidst the glitter let us see and hear the very ordinary

that proclaims Christ is born in us this holiday and

that allows us to make of this Christmas a HOLY DAY.

ALLELUIA!

The years in Drexel Hill reflect a travel bug that occurred with family that led us to understand much about the world beyond our country. It gave all of the family a new perspective as we learned first-hand about the customs, the beauty, and the needs of people around the world. Our Timeshare opportunities were an easy way to absorb other places. Such vacations were limited with the family, but found full expression over the years when Ralph and I covered most of the continents of the world. What a blessing for us! These were happy, wonderful years for our family. All kinds of growth took place within our lives and in the church we served. Ralph's and my love was something that our children absorbed. Visible love gave them a way to understand how important love was as a foundation for a happy home.

Family changed again when Joyce went off to college and to be on her own. We trusted that all of the family, home, and work experiences would go with her to enclose her with love. The time had come for us to move to Ontario, California.

ONTARIO, CALIFORNIA - 1973

When the call came to be senior pastor of the First Baptist Church of Ontario, California, this once again, caused upheaval and change in the family. Fourteen years had given us deep roots in Pennsylvania in home, work and family. All these would be changed. Following God's leading for both of us (our partnership in ministry and in love continued). After open discussion with the children, Ralph agreed to accept the call of this pastorate. Now we had to do serious planning that included each member of the family.

Joyce was away at college in Rhode Island and still had two years to complete her degree. She decided that she would like to move to California and further her studies. Keith was finishing his high school in June of the year and he chose to move with the family and find himself in new ways. I would terminate my employment with the Baptists at the national offices. All of these factors were a part of the decision that allowed Ralph to move in April, alone, to his new charge. I would stay in Pennsylvania to allow Keith to finish high school and for Joyce to complete her time at the University of Rhode Island. This schedule allowed us time to make arrangements for movers, selling the other car in the family, and time to find a home in Ontario, CA. I made a trip to California in May and while there we purchased our first major home in Ontario. Ralph was there to oversee the legal matters and to have it ready for the whole family to occupy it on arrival. Decisions about schools, work for the children and me, and so many other things were to await our settling into a new community.

On June 4, 1959, the family (Ralph had flown back to help with last minute closing details and to drive with us across the country). We packed into our car and started out across the country with so many unknowns for all of us.

This move had ramifications with family, as well. An entire continent was to separate us from the Brown family and its many relationships. We hoped that deep friendships and love would survive the separation and we would learn new ways of being in touch with one another. Love could reach across the miles containing all of us in family.

We found, that with all the changes that we did need time for relaxation and personal renewal that would come from setting time aside to just be. This poem about summer lifts up that need. Summer was an occasion for my pen to make its way to a page. *Summering* is a poem that tells a bit about home life in the Lightbody family and reflects some of the look and feel of this home with its yard and gardens.

SUMMERING

Summer is sibilant, listen to its sounds:

    Sitting – Standing

My mate and I sit on lounge chairs,

    a perfectly matched pair in my garden.

I stand in the garden pool and feel the water cool -

    relaxation – WOW!

    Sweating – Sweltering

sweltering temperatures – 100 or more,

this has gone on for day four -

    too much too much!

Sweat runs down in rivulets on this glass,

    on my face it sets and I am hot!

    Sipping – Supping

    I try to beat the heat as I sip cool icy tea

    and wish for a place to be oh so cool!

    The barbeque smoke tells me that

        supping good food will soon be a time to meet with friends!

    Sunning – Shading

    I seek the sun for vitamin D,

    but not too much for me; oh mercy me!

    I seek the shade so that I can be a reader,

        to be free, ah! this is summer repose!

    Simmering – Shimmering

    Even in the summer heat offering;

    some days are only simmering

>   oh what days!
>   I feel and see the heat shimmering
>   in August rays and globules of being
>   in the world about me!
> Summering is sibilant! Summering is full of promise!
> Summering is just time to be!

Ralph did his usual wonderful work in leading the congregation, being a pastor to all, both in the church and in the community. In addition, he served as Adjunct Faculty at the Baptist Seminary located in nearby Covina, CA. Rebuilding a small house on the property, that we used to house a refugee family, had its usual demands on time and wisdom, acquired from the past pastorates. At this point, we felt that we were professionals in the matter of building something new into the life of the various congregations. Such building was also an education for the church members and required real financial sharing. Ralph continued his ecumenical work and interfaith passions while here. In this time I went back and finished my Bachelor's degree, having a double major: psychology and sociology, (obviously having value as I worked in ministry), before starting to work full time. Work for me was in a position as Executive Director of the Pomona Valley Council of Churches with offices in nearby Pomona. I worked on my MA in Values from San Francisco Theological School, all the while working full time for the Council of Churches.

This work was to be my ministry for eight productive years, dealing with actions for housing, food serving, refugees, and church programs reaching across eleven communities with 41 churches. The Council worked with many church and social service agencies to offer even more help to all people therein. In addition to my administrative duties,

I helped with organizing small groups, as I had done in all my previous service ministries to particularize the kinds of service needed.

I continued to write poetry, many, many letters, and a monthly column for our newsletter. I was called on frequently to preach sermons in some of the local churches, as a part of my duties with the Council; my writing has now taken on the spoken word. Somehow all of this seemed an answer to God's call and was for me a time of happiness. One of the major concerns, for me personally and for our Council, was the matter of justice, care of the poor, and peace. This was a conscious activity within the member churches. To that end, I wrote this poem:

LIGHTING CANDLES

One candle can barely pierce the darkness.
One candle is not enough to illumine much,
 but it is a ray of HOPE.
Today I light a candle asking for that HOPE:
  for all the famine struck and hungry people
  in so many places in our world
Two candles will give a lovely light.
The radiance of two candles encircles more,
  where more are gathered, there is LOVE.
Today I light a candle asking for LOVE :
  that it may be found by all the people in our world
  who need to remember the poor, the elderly,
   those with no jobs, those who are in despair.
Three candles help to banish the darkness
  in the long reaches over the desert spaces
  as strangers come to the birth of the holy child.

Three candles can become a symbol
> of the light that God brought to our world.

Today I light a candle that expresses my JOY
> that we are all encompassed by God's love.
> shown to us in Jesus Christ
> and that there is enough to share with all.

More candles, too numerous to count
> will illuminate an entire world,
> will gather humanity with upraised arms
>> into a time of PEACE.

Today I light a candle that PEACE may become a reality
> for all the war torn countries and
> anywhere people cry out for justice.

May we come together, with millions of lighted candles
> to commit ourselves to becoming God's instruments
> to bring God's light to our world.

Our ranch style home, located about three blocks from the church, suited us perfectly, even including shelter space for Joyce and Keith, while they made plans for the upcoming fall season when schools would begin. Joyce entered the University of California at Santa Barbara in the College of Creative Studies to complete her degree. She moved into housing there, but knew that her home was open and waiting for her. During the summer months she worked at waitressing in a nearby city.

Keith applied at the local junior college and did a semester there. During the summer he worked in a local business. Within a year he enlisted in the army and did his tour of duty in nearby forts in California and then spent another tour in Germany.

Both of the children married and moved out of our home and

created homes of their own. They always knew that our home was there for them. Joyce married Tom who had two children from a previous marriage. We became grandparents with ten and twelve year old wonderful young people. Tom's family was Jewish and so we absorbed what was beautiful in both traditions. Keith married Arlene and they brought Brian into the world, adding to our grandparent status. With the advent of these children, we always had holidays together, keeping the bonds of family tighter.

The Brown family, my parents and my brother's family all moved to California during our years in Ontario – my parents to Ontario and my brother to Carmel, CA. Those ties were only strengthened in new ways.

Family now had many extensions with all the variety of relationships; with people being so involved in movement, business, schools and individual activities. Holidays, especially Christmas, needed a central location and it was in the Lightbody home. We now represented diversity in faith. We tried to help all see the importance of faith and service in a needy world and where a loving God was leading us. It was in these matters that I resumed writing poetry for home and family consumption.

JOURNEY TO CHRISTMAS

Christmas is about journeying —
>   the slow plodding donkey,
>   carrying the mother and child,
>   not yet born on the road to Bethlehem.
> The measured tread punctuated by
>   the walking stick and Joseph
>   finding the uncertain path to Bethlehem.
> The undulating walk of the three camels,

carrying nobility, carrying those
who dared to follow a star to Bethlehem.
Out on the hillside, the lonely men
sit in the cold, tending flocks, and
rise to find the one, who is only a tiny baby;
they go to Bethlehem.
Plodding, plodding this is my time spent
in this lifetime of journeying.
Now an elder in my life,
frequently the last leaf on a tree,
among my friends and even in family.
I seek to find my later roads to my own Bethlehem.

In the midst of all the angst in the world, the divisions, unending hatred sown in many places, locally, in America, and worldwide, I count those years as good. Those years were opportunities for the Lightbody and Brown families, plus Joyce and Keith's families to find serenity, joy and amazing love. It was a time of celebration as we continued to seek God's will.

VALLEJO, CALIFORNIA – 1981

In 1981, with Joyce and Keith and families on their own, we accepted the Call of the First Baptist Church of Vallejo, California to become their pastor (I count myself as a significant part of the ministry of that church). Vallejo is a suburb of San Francisco. All of our ministries have been around large metropolises which speaks of the reason why social justice issues have always been vital to us. Our home was a California ranch style house and was of a kind that invited people to visit us. It had room for our children and other family when they would come to visit; a wonderful peace when family was just the two of us. Ralph continued to be a superb pastor and also served as Adjunct Faculty at the Baptist Seminary located in Berkeley.

It was here that the building part of our life, which had so encompassed all of our ministries. Was again put to use. In this case it meant working on a small house on the property and doing earthquake prevention. Our brick church, with its tall tower, had to meet California's standards and be earthquake proofed.

My parents moved to a new home in a retirement community in Auburn, California one year after our move to Vallejo. My brother still lived in the Carmel/Monterey area and my children were in their own homes in Southern California. Now family extended from the southern part of California to the middle, to the Bay Area and to the northern part of the state. Dad died in Auburn in 1986. Ralph conducted the memorial service in Auburn. I spoke for the family in deeply felt words of thanks for my father. Here is an excerpt from that time.

> *Today we celebrate the life of an ordinary man. He was husband, father, grandfather, great grandfather. He did none of the things that make for fame or fortune. He lived life simply, but in ways that affirmed his values of decency, honor and caring. He shared with us his hard work, his experience, his love. He was a man of God.*

Mother remained in Auburn for several years. This was the beginning of a significant change in family, caused by death in the nuclear family; a sad time not only for Ralph and me, but also for our children and the grandchildren for whom he was a presence in their lives.

Work for me was serving as the Administrator of Calvary Presbyterian Church in San Francisco. This was my five day a week job, with occasionally having to be there on weekends. Commuting has always meant that I traveled to my work from our home in any of the Baptist pastorates. However, this commute gave our family of two wonderful opportunities to stretch our horizons. We become enamored of the city of San Francisco. We were a part of a widespread interreligious group, one that had been always a part of the way Ralph and I did ministry.

After six years of new friends, new tasks and gratitude for Calvary church, I left that position and became one of the administrative team for RIDES for BAY AREA COMMUTERS. This was a ridesharing group that put passengers into a common carpool related to their area as they looked for rides into San Francisco. My duties were in several areas within the company: Human Resources, and publications and printing issues within the company.

Building, even there, became a part of my life. Our offices needed to move and I was the person working out the details of new office space: interior design and planning the physical use of the office space. This work received approval by our Board.

My days were full, but interesting. I handled this full time job, along with my volunteer tasks; entertaining, creating small groups, writing, and teaching adult church school classes; as well as other tasks within our church. My work with the denominational magazine, *Crusader* continued for a short time while in Vallejo.

My writing took a new direction. I used my limited free time to indulge in serious writing. My first book was published while we were in Vallejo. It was entitled: ***FAITH is the JOURNEY.*** That book was a series of essays telling about my experiences in commuting to my position in San Francisco. It was well received by my church, within the city and my work at Calvary, as well. Culling faith thoughts while experiencing travel and my environment made for a deepening of my faith.

My daily trek to San Francisco became a large headache with the earthquake of 1988 when the Bay Bridge collapsed. This caused me to find alternative ways to get to the city. I had just gone over the bridge on my way home shortly before the collapse of the bridge. I was very fortunate that day. I did find alternative ways to go: over two other bridges or taking a ferry and finding surface transportation to get to my work. After a six month rerouting, life became normal again.

To talk of Faith Matters in this parish would seem to encompass all that had gone before, as well as finding new resources for our family of two and the ministries we served. I was grateful for the love of God that surrounded us through all of these years. Our own love grew, even as we were sharing it with so many more people. Faith matters.

We made a turn of the journey when we believed that God was leading Ralph to consider retirement and leaving this particular ministry. I had retired from my full-time employment earlier. For a year or two I did some consulting work with some local churches on administrative work and development of small groups within their churches. We were now ready to listen for God's call and to decide where our lives, within God's will, would lead our journey in these later years.

CLAREMONT, CALIFORNIA – 1991

In the years we were in Ontario in the 1970's, we had become acquainted with a wonderful retirement community, called Pilgrim Place, in nearby Claremont. It offered three levels of care.

We had placed our names on the waiting list for the time when we would be ready to move there. Pilgrim Place was a community of retired Christian workers, including missionaries, pastors, YMCA and YWCA workers, and those who worked in seminaries and in church related vocations. The time had come! We left Vallejo in 1991, now only a family of two, ready for next steps in the journey.

Family now was changing once again. With our move so far from my mother, we found a place for her in a retirement community in Upland, a near neighbor. This allowed us to care for her more easily. She came, after a few years, to live in our community's Skilled Nursing Facility. She lived there until her death in 1997 at the age of 91. Ralph led her memorial service and again I put into words the homily, telling of this amazing woman. Here it is in excerpted form.

> *We want to celebrate Mother's life, all of it. Not just the loving person who taught us about living, about God, about values and service, but the person she became when her deafness and blindness left her isolated in her own world. This changed her into a person with great needs. In this time, she offered us the opportunity to give back to her. We hope, even in her confused state, she knew she was loved. We celebrate the creative years of her life and ministry among us. We celebrate all the years she was with us and we rejoice because she lived.*

Now moving back into the home, work, family familiarity; in retirement, we found life to be filled with new challenges. Our children and their families were again within easy driving distance and we had real fellowship with Joyce and Keith and families. Family now included a new host of members as we brought into our loving familial concern, those within the Pilgrim Place community.

We entered into a new church affiliation, as members of the

congregation, at the Claremont United Methodist Church. Here it was our pleasure and a continuing response to our call from God to find service in this, our final church home.

Home was uniquely different. We were fortunate that Pilgrim Place gave us the opportunity to pay for the building of our home within the community at 601 Harrison Avenue. The fact of building throughout our marriage, meant that once again we were encased with architects. This was to be our first brand new home. We had lived in homes that were 125 years old, sixty years old, forty eight years old, nine years old, and two years old. This was a building with our personal features, made to suit our needs. In this home, Ralph and I lived for twenty-four years. This house spoke of home to the many persons we entertained there, to the many visitors, and to family.

Following Mother's death, I wrote my second book entitled ***REFLECTIONS on CARING for an AGING PARENT:*** this was a series of letters that I wrote but never did send. They told of her life in these later years and how it impacted me. It was a lovingly told story; both of good and not so good times and issues that we faced in her remaining years. The book was understood to be a guide for others who might have to focus on similar issues.

Ralph did a year-long interim as pastor in a church in Gardena and I did a nine month interim as Director at the Inland Valley Council of Churches. Now we were both on a commute. Our other "work" took place within the Pilgrim Place community where we served in places of leadership and on many committees on a volunteer basis. My penchant for entertaining and starting small groups had many opportunities in our community. As always, it was rewarding and joyous work.

Spiritually our joint faith journey took us into new byways, even as we sustained the faith that had led us through so many years of life. The Pilgrim Place community was and is a place of vibrant faith, where social action and a just social order are integral to the community. This caused growth in our personal faith.

Having more time for meditation and study helped me to absorb the many difficulties imposed by our aging concerns, those occurring within family and in the wider world. Where was God's call to lead us? All of these times of the deep probing of God's call led to my moving into the next chapter – the CHANGED JOURNEY.

I Am Audrey Brown Lightbody

Child of God,
older pilgrim, still a faith seeker
ever journeying into the new
and vital life within God's plan.

The Changed Journey

The Later Years

I Am Audrey
*still a Child of God,
a person who carries within me
all that has been a part of me;
whose family, work, home and faith
have been and continue to be
the journey.*

The jigsaw pieces have been fitted together, showing the life of one woman in its many facets – its many parts of the journey. It is close to the finalization of the puzzle. There is only one person seeking to find how to enclose a life. To put in the final piece will ensure that there are no missing pieces.

As I deal with these later years, I have left the story of each of the various parishes and movement of life and return to the first manner in which we looked at the various aspects that make up life patterns. It seems appropriate to look back and find unique ways that differ from the beginnings and this time leading to the ending. This, also, is the time in which I shall share the deep creativity of the family: Ralph, Joyce, and Keith.

Family– A Changed Journey

What is there about a family?

What does being in a family mean?

Family is continually in change; additions and subtractions,

> *change within its members as the years come*
>> *and go,*
> *change within the outreach among its members,*
> *changing perceptions about the place within the family of all who make up the family unit.*

Ultimate change assures us of God's love.

I was not the only writer in the family. Each member had a developed creativity streak that showed itself in both the work they did and the sharing of themselves in unique ways. Here are brief examples from my husband and children.

Ralph

This man, my husband, shared his creative vision regularly with countless people as he prepared and delivered sermons on a weekly basis, led meetings wisely, and wrote numerous articles. He loved music, enjoyed playing the piano and leading song fests. However, one of his unique creative talents was in writing hymnody. While he wrote a number of hymns, I share with you the hymn, **CREATIVE GOD WE GATHER,** which became the central hymn at the biannual meeting of the American Baptist Churches USA in one of the later years of his life.

CREATOR GOD, WE GATHER

Creator God, we gather to seek your peace and will.
We stand in awe and wonder; we're from your bounty filled.
The glories of creation; the majesty of love;
The thrill of spirit power all coming from above.

We need your presence daily to guide us on our way
A constant fresh renewal to fight the dark away.
God grant us your empowering as we turn to you.
God, may our opening hearts stir and rise, your will to do.

We reel with pain and anguish in our world's tragic times:
The hungry and battered; hates, acts from passions blind,
All form a smothering circle that crushes hope, dims light
And causes us to wander from visions of peace and right.

Renew Thy Church, O Savior, to be in these rough days,
A clarion of justice, a place of open praise,
Where all your children gather acknowledging our sin,
And drawing from your power new strength from deep within.

Joyce

Creating art and music were the major part of her life from her college years onward. She has taught for many years at Otis College of Art and Design and has also taught courses at UCLA, as well as at the California Institute of the Arts – all of these in California. This was her week by week work. In reality, being an artist and musician, was and is, the way in which she sees herself. This is how many in the art world know her. She is an established artist, doing conceptual art and making collages that combine her interests. She has created musical and art displays that work together in her world. She has had her work in many art shows, in some business offices and in some private collections. Joyce has created musical compositions that have been done in presentation pieces before audiences and created CD's of her music. She was commissioned to do this combination of music and an art exhibit for the carillon at the University of California, Santa Barbara.

I have shown her creative talents below, as found in a CD cover and art. I have included a picture of an art piece that is typical of her work, but does not define her many styles of art. In addition to that I share a piece that was created for Ralph's and my anniversary. It combines her musical idea of word values, color, numbers, and poetry. It is written phonetically and therefore may not be easy to understand. It is really the story of growing up in our home. Listed below is a translation:

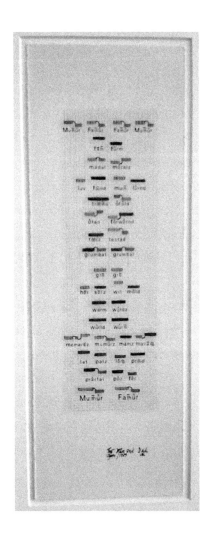

Mother, Father - Father, Mother
faith firm
model morals
love found, much learned
often forewarned
rules tested
grumble, grumble
grow, grow
whole souls will mold
warm words
world worth
memories, Mummers,
mom's meringues
laugh, pals, lomg proud
prayerful pause
for
Mother, Father

A representation of Joyce's art and a CD cover of her songs

Keith

As an adult and a family man, Keith worked at a variety of employments after completing his army service. As a lover of animals he worked with the Upland SPCA; this is where he met his wife. He then worked for a moving company and was sent to a school by the company for learning specialized skills. He worked for them for fifteen years. He ended his work employment with a Petroleum Transportation company as their night dispatcher for ten years.

In all this time, he used his creative abilities in coaching Little League Teams at all levels. He was active in Alcoholics Anonymous, where he led people into becoming clean and sober. However his real creativity came in writing poetry. It is amazing that this man, who as a student, couldn't deal with the abstract, would find his real ability in writing meaningful poetry. I list two of his poems:

SIMPLY ME

I wanna cry and sometimes die,
or maybe just run and hide
for my emotions are just lost inside.

Life's a game, but just the same
there's gotta be pain before we gain.
As we grow, we must always know
that God loves us all, don't you know?

I wanna win in this game of life
because to lose sight will end my life.

It's what you make, not what you take,
you gotta give, if you want to live.

I'm a scared little boy,
crying in a man's body
for my emotions are just lost inside.
He's coming out – he wants to be free.
He just wants to say, "Hey, look at me.
I just simply wanted to be free."

I know for today that I can make it
even if I have to fake it.

Simply me.

SIMPLY YOU

As I look into the windows of your soul
I can see there's a lot to be told.

Struggling hard to make ends meet,
one who can't easily accept defeat.

With a heart of gold and a smile untold,
compassionate and sincere, she covers her fear
Straightforward and honest, no room for gain,

Moving cautiously, she's going through change.
Yes looking into windows a story unfolds:
through each one, a different tale is told.

and what I see is
SIMPLY YOU

The journey was changing in so many ways for each of the family. These changes occurred while we still lived in our home in Pilgrim Place. Ralph developed heart problems and his ventricular fibrillation meant that he was not always aware of when his strength would be depleted. Even in the midst of this, he continued doing too many work tasks. The need for more care required me to start making alterations in our living style. It was a gift of love to the man whom I had loved for so long.

Immediate family was to change in these years. Keith divorced and became the parent with whom his son lived. Also in this period of time, but several years later, Joyce's marriage ended and she set out on her own journey changes. My brother and his wife, Edie, moved to Oregon.

Death became an all too familiar companion. My beloved Ralph died in 2003 at the age of 77. Who he was, was attested to by the numbers of people at his memorial service. Many people, who were former members from several pastorates, as well as a host of friends who loved this man, witnessed, by their presence, to his power in their lives.

It was my joy to share a very personal tribute about this child of

God at this service. Both my daughter and son spoke their own very personal words at his service, a Celebration of Life. While there were many more words said by me, I give you some of my words that speak of the deepest part of this man:

> Ralph was a lover of me through the years of adventuring into new areas of love, joy, sadness and grief. His love was not in a narrow context, but enveloped all he knew. His love of God was the bedrock of his loving life.
>
> His was the pastor/shepherd heart, for all people whose lives he touched. Out of that heart of love, he became an advocate for righting wrongs and for leading people to see God's will.
>
> Ralph was a reconciler. His gentle way was to bring healing. He wanted to bring wholeness to people and situations. He never wanted to be great; he just let, who he was deep inside, speak to all those whose lives he touched. Today should not be a time of sadness, but a celebration of a life lived in God's will and shared with us. ALLELUIA!

Life was never to be the same and now I moved into new changes in the journey. Having already lost both my parents and my beloved husband, next I gave my son into God's care. Keith, died in 2005 of lung and brain cancer. He was fifty years old. Children should not predecease their parents. This was a tragedy. I became the speaker at Keith's memorial service that told of his life. That life had not been easy because he chose a pathway that led to addictions, but also led to recovery and the example he set for many of his friends. He was a loving and loved son. Some of the words from his service:

> As a child and into adulthood, Keith was a charmer of all he met. He was a father who loved his son

and tried to teach him worthwhile values. Because of his own example of a youth that was troubled, he tried to lead his son into a meaningful adulthood. His success is attested to by the way, Brian, his son, has taken loving care of his father through his last illness.

My last words have to do with his deep spirituality, and the way he shared himself in writing and friendships. During the days of nursing home care, I have been humbled by the love, respect and deep caring of the staff, his many friends, and certainly by family.

A special memory I have is that since the cancer was diagnosed, I have touched and caressed him and hope that through my touch, I have communicated God's loving touch as he moved into God's everlasting love. Thank God for such a man.

In 2006 my brother, now living in Redmond, Oregon, developed cancer and died in that year. He was 76. I went to Oregon for my brother's Celebration of Life service, in which I was again, the family spokesperson. Bob was a gifted person: an artist, entrepreneur and storekeeper and owner of several stores he developed. He was a good man. These are some of my words at his service:

I remember my brother, not as a famous man, but as a man who cared for his family and friends; one who loved beauty and tried to make the world he knew into a safe and lovely environment. Creativity followed him into his business ventures, making beauty within his stores, his home, and among his friends. He was a man who trusted his life into God's eternity. I remember and celebrate the life

> *of one we shall all miss, knowing that nothing is*
> *lost on the breath of God.*

Three deaths within a three year period took its toll on my life. These three deaths meant that the basic three men in my life were gone. Suddenly, I was the matriarch of both Brown and Lightbody families. Immediate family now was down to two, my daughter, Joyce, and me, as the remainder of our nuclear family.

Having been the spokesperson for so much of my family, at the times of their deaths, I need to say some words about Joyce, now my constant source of family. She continues to be a much loved and loving daughter, even as she goes about her busy life as a professor at two colleges. She also works as a therapist in assisting those who are among the poorest to find stability and joy in their lives. She is a treasure.

On the occasion of her sixty-fourth birthday, I penned these words for her and since I probably will not be alive to speak at her memorial, I hope these words may make clear the wonderful woman she has always been.

THERE WAS A CHILD

There was a child – a baby girl
    with big brown eyes and strawberry blond hair,
    who held out her arms, seeking love.
There was a family – who had love to share
    who clasped the child and
    poured out through hugs and kisses,
     enough love to enclose the child,
     and then become a part of family.
There was a child – the baby girl,

who secure in family love, learned what it was

  to walk and talk and know the shared love

     in home and daily living.

There was a child, now moved beyond the toddler stage,

  who learned at school and church

  and from others who would share in that outgoing love.

There was a child who continued to reach out her arms,

  still seeking to find herself,

  to learn that there was a whole world

  that would be a part of a growing life.

There was a teen-ager, still with the big brown eyes,

  and a hair and face to match her years,

  who has grown in knowledge,

  who learned about her body, mind and spirit,

    about her unique self as she approached adulthood.,

    and still stretched out her arms,

      giving and receiving love.

There was a young adult, who found herself still within family,

  but moving beyond - in friends,

  in others who challenged her,

  into a world of art and music, and care for others.

There is a woman, who stands alone,

  who has amassed knowledge, burnished her skills,

  who has many friends;

  who offers herself to the big world out there,

    and still holds out her arms, seeking and receiving love.

There is a woman who has lived through many cycles of life –

  always reaching out for love in new forms,

  finding love that brought a new family into being,

  offering to share herself and give love

to a younger generation.

That time of life was a cycle completed.

In it she knew great love and,

now, sadness at its ending.

There is a woman who is known in the art world:

gallery promotions, signature art within some businesses,

exhibits of art in many venues, some fame.

She was out there for all to see as she, through her art

stretched out her arms, through color and design,

to awaken new ideas and challenge all to think more deeply.

There is a woman who shared her love of music:

by writing scores, by cutting CDs,

by creating performance pieces of joyous melodies,

and making music that rings out in a carillon,

thus broadcasting herself in her own unique styles.

There is a woman who shares her love through teaching:–

a host of students have received this love as this woman

has reached out her arms to enable others

to find beauty in form and design.

By challenging all within her reach to go deeper,

and become their own unique selves.

There is a woman whose arms keep reaching out to others

through therapeutic sessions as she guides

those in deep need to believe in themselves and

seek a better life.

There is a woman I am proud to call my daughter

who shares her love with me for all my days.

2006 became a year in which I focused on finding myself as

Audrey – just as I was in the beginning. This is not a disclaimer of family or all of the other names by which I was known, but spoke of my inner need to be me in my simplest form. This fact challenged my faith and caused me to think more deeply about where God was leading me in my later years. This poem speaks to that time period. Following the poem, I will move on, from family to look at the aspects of home, work and faith matters.

GOD LISTENED

God listened, God is listening, God will listen …
Listen God –
>   while I tell you of things that really matter to me;
>   while I tell you of hurting people, of my hurt;
>   while I carefully give you an expurgated version of my weaknesses.

Listen God –
>   because I want answers that clear up all the mysteries,
>   because I need to believe that someone cares,
>   because someone must hear my cries.

God listened through all the days of life gone by.
God is listening today, even though I have not found the answers.
God will listen if I open my heart and my being
to receive God's flood of lovingkindness.
God, indwelling me, demands I be a listener too.
>   Have I listened?

Do I really care enough to take my time?
I have become so busy with so many things that
>   when a friend wants to tell me of her needs,
>   I have passed by so fast I could not hear.

I am afraid that if I listen

    demands, I cannot meet will be made of me.

    I have not always learned to listen with a heart of love.

God listened, God is listening, I will listen.

God, indwelling me, demands I listen too

Home – A Changed Journey

What is a home? What changes a house into a home?

    A house where love flows constantly is a home,

    no matter where it is located,

    for all who live within its bounds.

Home allows us to become the persons God calls us to be!

Home was still the same place, where I lived for twelve more years after Ralph's death, as a single person. The loss of Ralph and his love in my life made an indelible mark on all of this part of my journey. In the time between other tasks and family, who still spend the holidays with me (how blessed I was to have them with me during these years). My home became a safe place for new people coming to Pilgrim Place to find friendship and share life stories that enriched us all.

Another major change occurred in my life when I decided that twelve years alone in a home that was too large for a single woman. It required me to give thought to finding a smaller place. Our Pilgrim Place community has Assisted Living as well as a Skilled Nursing Facility. I made the decision to move into the Friendship Court part of the Pitzer Assisted Living facilities. A goodly part of that decision was my age – almost ninety. This was to be my home for the immediately foreseeable future. I embraced it with joy.

I could not leave my Harrison Street home just as a point blank act. I felt the need to do a ritual on leaving that home that would go on to other families. I have included the ritual that I used at the time. In that ritual I mention many of the happenings that are also under family. The candle lighting service, held with a few of my friends, was one part of the preparation for the journey into the unknown.

RITUAL FOR LEAVING 601 HARRISON AVENUE

Ralph and I came to Pilgrim Place in January of 1991. We elected to pay for the building of a new home at 601 Harrison Avenue. We lived in a rental of Pilgrim Place for several months, and watched the house being built. This was the first brand new house we had lived in in our 54 years of marriage. We had lived in homes that were 125 years old and then in varying age years of houses – the youngest being two years old, until we came to this house. We arranged it to fit our retired lifestyle years. It became a place where we would put our own unique mark. It became a place of love. Here is the ritual:

I want to begin this time of ritual with the singing of the hymn: This is a Day of New Beginnings. It speaks of my next steps in the journey.

<u>I light a candle for our beginning in this home</u>

In our 24 years we have done landscaping, made new arrangements, figured out a way to be at home, independent and yet a part of this intentional community, as we journeyed on into new ways of living. As the years passed, our life journeys continued in this house.

I light a candle for the journey in our Pilgrim way

Over the years the inner decorations have changed, the landscape is different as we conserve water. It is not the same house, although the exterior is the same. The friends this house has known have been different over the years, and yet it is still a part of the Pilgrim Place community. How will it fit into newness of new people?

I light a candle for the guests who have known the hospitality of this house.

Over the 24 years we, and then I alone, have welcomed into this house so many friends, so many new Pilgrims with food, fellowship and friendship. Our lives and now mine, have been enriched because of the initial sharing that led to deep caring for one another.

I light a candle and remember my loved ones, alive in God's care.

Not all has been joyous in this house – death has been within its walls. After twelve years of shared marriage in Pilgrim Place, my beloved Ralph moved on to God's eternity. His presence is in the walls, the flowers and remembrances as I have lived here alone. In those years too, my son, who spent many hours and days here, finished his journey.

I light a candle for change

And now I leave 601 Harrison Avenue and all that is familiar and all that is me within its walls. I leave the stained glass window that proclaims our faith, and wonder what it will mean to a new family that will come in. They will not know who birthed it into existence and that it was a link to our previous home. May God bless the lives of those who follow – this is my prayer.

I light the candle that ends this Lightbody home

And now I look ahead to moving still within Pilgrim Place to a simpler living, to a place where others have been before. I wonder what the walls of this new place will share with me as I make that place my own. How many years will I be there to make myself comfortable and know I am in God's plan?

I light a different candle for showing a new way and pray that God who holds all creation in loving hands will lead me in the way ahead.

I want to conclude this time together with another hymn: In the Midst of New Dimensions. My prayer is that we all may feel God's healing power for today, and know the faith that God will bless both my and your journeys as we move into a new part of the journey.

I thank you, my friends for sharing in this vital time for me, and pray that your lives will also be filled with happy memories of your years in various homes. AMEN

Home, Work, Family, and Faith Matters - A New Call

Writing poetry did not change because of new home facilities. I recognized the concerns that come with giving up a dearly loved home and also giving up driving my car. To that end, I wrote two humorous poems that tell it like it is today.

ON BEING OLD

I am an OLD lady – Yes!
I am OLD, that is a fact!
I say this in tones so BOLD!

I know I have aged because

    I live in a retirement community

    where I have learned just to be one of the FOLD

I have gained many things in all my years of living,

    but not much GOLD!

    I have spent years with many things, but now I wonder

    if there are any I should HOLD!

    I have grown in many ways, tried to be unique,

        but still I find I am in the same old MOLD!

I have become an accumulator, but now I ponder

        if there is something to be SOLD?

I have put down these thoughts and consider

        if there is a story that should be TOLD?

I recognize at last, these thoughts

        belong to someone OLD!

ODE TO A CAR

I gave up my CAR! I gave up my CAR! Now I had a new concern:

    how was I to get to all locations and events that are a part of my life?

I had to find a CAR or CARS with drivers that would take me where I wanted to go;

    I had to find friends who would share their CARS with me, at my request.

So, dear friends, I turned to you and you shared your CARS with me:

    I want you to know how much your CARS have meant to me,

    so I wrote this "ODE TO A CAR."

There are certain things that a CAR is not:

    In my case, not in a CAR(AVAN), nor was it a CAR(AWAY) seed,

    nor would I hold a CAR(BINE), nor would it be a CAR(BUNCLE).

It is not a CAR(BOHYDRATE), although it uses its own fattening fuel.

There are some things it does hold, unique to each maker: a CAR(CASS).

If improperly used, it might produce a CAR(CINOGEN).

The user may need to use a CAR(D) to keep it running

And you may hope that it doesn't become a CAR(DIAC) problem for you.

Now here is something that may fit in two categories:

The driver may take CAR(E) and be both CAR(EFUL) or CARE(LESS)

or one could be CAR(EFREE).

There is no doubt – one needs a vehicle to carry CAR(GO) – oh those bags of groceries.

Another need is to have CAR(ING) friends – and that you are!

There is also music: CAR(OL) and CAR(ILLON) that can be enjoyed within its confines.

CAR(PET) is in the vehicle to deaden the sound, and if the passengers CAR(P) too much, you can give them a CAR(PETBAG) and send them on their way.

There are many vehicles by which you can be CAR(RIED): CAR(RIAGE) or CAR(T).

Finally, my friends: there is a word that sums it all up: People who CAR(VE) out time

to help a poor damsel in distress, and never count the cost of CAR usage, their time and the sharing of friendship: this is a sign of great C(H)ARACTER. You are WONDERFUL.

WORK – A Changed Journey

What is work? Why do I work? Is work a necessity in life?

Work is a way of helping others in their journey,

> *It allows me to be God's worker wherever the journey leads.*
>
> *Is work a necessity in my life? I say "yes" because*
>
> *work gives meaning in my inmost being as a child of God.*

Work now was only the volunteer kind, as had been true after the completion of my interim position. I continued doing committee tasks even through these years. In 2006 I became the Moderator of the residents' group, using my administrative skills and my ability to be a helper to many others. This position put me on the Board of Pilgrim Place, giving me the opportunity to speak for the residents on matters of policy for this non-profit Continuing Care Retirement Community.

2006 was the year in which I published a book of poetry, entitled **FRAGMENTED SENSES.** Once again my writing focused on fragments, this time they related to the various senses that make up the lives of all people everywhere.

I published another book that shared more of my journey. This book published in 2012 was entitled **ORDINARY FRAGMENTS.** This book was concerned with "Ordinary Time," a period of time in the Christian year. The fragments were a group of daily meditations to be used at that time of the year. It was my joy to use it with my support group of women who blessed my life in ways too numerous to mention.

Faith Matters – A Changed Journey

What is faith? How do I acquire it?
What does my faith tell me
in this new place in my solitary journey?
I have moved into a place where I do so,
trusting in God's promises.
I bring the faith lessons from so many persons
that have merged into a unity in me,
trusting that all of the seeds planted
have grown into a strong life-giving force
that will guide me into joy in these later years.
Faith, hope, love, and service are gifts in my life;
are a part of me in trust from God.
Faith and belief are held deep within my life.

In 2017, at the age of 90, I wrote another book, entitled, ***JOURNALING THE BYWAYS OF LIFETIME JOURNEYS***. This book, written in journal form as fiction, asks the reader to consider many of life's pathways which seem like byways. They are a necessary part of one's lifetime. The various senses are part of the growth that leads all persons into mature adulthood.

As I move further into my nineties, life takes on a degree of sameness. Home and work remain much the same with moments of bright color as I become challenged to find my way into some new area of God's plan. One such occasion presented itself when I was asked to speak to a circle of a woman's group at my church. Preparation for this time led me into thinking about circles, thus the cause for this poem that fits into faith matters. It demands enlarging my faith to be even more inclusive.

CIRCLES

What is a circle? What does it take to make a circle?
  Must a circle be round? Are there circles within circles?
How do we create circles?
  I sought answers from my lifetime journeys!
The fog was too heavy for the plane to land,
  so we circled round and round
  until there was a break in the encircling fog.
I walked the labyrinth and prayed
  in a circle of meditation within the larger circle,
  sending words to God even as my feet walked.
Circles of joy, made as we join in the dance, created to show praise
  on every continent, in every land; we become part
  of the dance of life – creating the wonder found in circles.
A circle, not really enclosed, as we join hands around the world:
  offering hands of different colors, of varied faiths
  that can reach out to bless a needy world.
Won't you join me by being a part of a circle
  which is inclusive, filled with joy, peace, and love.
  Let it begin in these moments.

Even as circles touched my inner life, so I must be open and alive to whatever challenges me to move from sameness into new pathways; to hear new Calls from God. I need to receive and give love to friends here, and friends far away, and even to a needy world. So, I look and walk without fear, and with the assurance of God's love, into my journey to the unknown.

I Am Audrey

Child of God

older pilgrim

still a faith seeker

who dares to walk an unknown pathway

that leads to life within God's plan.

Journey to the Unknown

The Years to Be

I Am Audrey

still a Child of God,

trying to be ready

for God's eternity

The last pieces have been added. Now the woman looks into the mists and wonders whether in eternity there will be new puzzles to de done with the hand of God to guide her.

This final fragment attempts to pull together an ending that fits what has gone before in the journey. The fragments have brought me to the point of entrusting my journey in a new and deeper commitment to God's love and call to lead me into the unknown.

As I plan for this journey, I will not need to pack, to find movers, to make arrangements for what is to be left in readiness during my time away. The breakdown into Family, Home, Work, and Faith Matters are a part of the journey that remains unknown.

I had a dream one night, in which I was part of a group that was tramping up a mountainous area, following a snowstorm. There was snow all around. In my dream I was separated from the rest of the group. I found myself sitting in a little niche, in the snow that had dirt that had been tracked from previous walkers. I sat in the niche and looked ahead to where I saw brightness, inviting areas to see even farther. Here I was still clinging to earthly areas, as seen by the dirt that had turned the snow into blackened areas. I realized that I wanted to move into the unknown area ahead, but could not move away from all that has been. This was a part of my journey to the unknown: seeing the glory up ahead, but not yet ready to move with unfaltering steps into the unknown. I go with hope that there are "no missing pieces."

I am open to God's call in uncertain ways for me, so I write some words that speak of the past, present, and future of my journey.

THE UNKNOWN

All of my life has had its unknown moments,
    until answers and directions
    have shown the way,
    until God has made the unknown, known
The past and present have happened;

now I stand at the future,

   still listening for God's call.

All of the renditions of Audrey are

   wrapped up in this woman

   who wants to walk with God

   into the unknown years.

Will I be attuned to hear God's slightest whisperings

   when my hearing is so far gone?

Will I see a clear pathway ahead

   when my eyes fall dimmer yet?

What can I do when my heart speaks out, calling for justice,

   when physical limitations keep me bound in place?

Will the faith, which has been an inner part of Audrey,

   be used to shape my world in the here and now?

Will it lead me in new ways of loving care?

Will I hear God call: Audrey, Audrey,

   and find a way to reach out my hand

   to clasp the hand of God;

   then to share the goodness of God's love

   with every neighbor that I see?

The unknown beckons; there is no choice.

I wait to answer God's call,

   as it leads to eternity.

ALLELUIA

ALLELUIA

ALLELUIA

AMEN

Lightning Source UK Ltd.
Milton Keynes UK
UKHW041352090119
335177UK00001B/3/P